We Are Fungi

CHRISTINE NISHIYAMA

Published by
Might Could Studios
100 6th St NE
Atlanta, GA 30308

www.mightcouldstudios.com

WE ARE Fungi

CHRISTINE might could NISHIYAMA

MUSHROOM
HUNTING DOG

Deep
inside
the damp,
dark forest,

MYCOLOGY
BOOK

hiding behind the
pine needles and twigs,
Can you see us?
Do you know us?

YEAST

We are some of the smallest living things on Earth.

2.4 MILE WIDE HONEY
FUNGUS COLONY IN OREGON

We are some of the biggest
living things on Earth.

We have pores and gills.
We have wrinkles and caps.

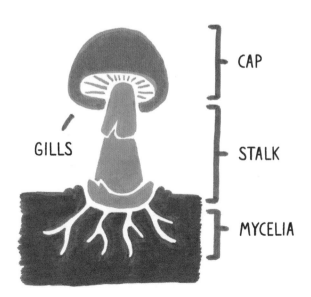

CAP

GILLS

STALK

MYCELIA

We are white and we are yellow.
We are brown and we are pink.

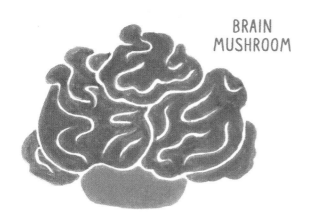

BRAIN
MUSHROOM

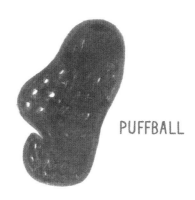

PUFFBALL

We look like slimy brains,

BOLETE

PINK OYSTER
MUSHROOM

and we look like strings of hair.

LION'S MANE
MUSHROOM

LEMON YELLOW
LAPIOTA

We climb high above.

And we slither down below.

We sprout up between dead leaves
beneath the forest floor.

And we invade the cheese forgotten
in your refrigerator door.

We grow and hide between your toes.

We come alive and raise your bread.

We also live...

COPROPHILOUS FUNGI

...in poop.

BIOLUMINESCENCE

FAIRY RING

We glow green in the dark of night,
and we commune in fairy rings.

We bulge when the air is dripping and damp.

We shrivel up when the air is parched and dry.

We have weird names like:

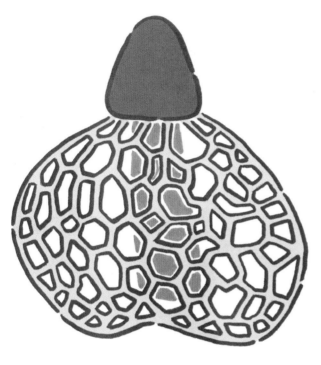

Veiled Lady,
(PHALLUS INDUSIATUS)

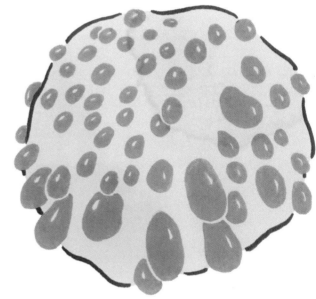

Bleeding Tooth,
(HYDNELLUM PECKII)

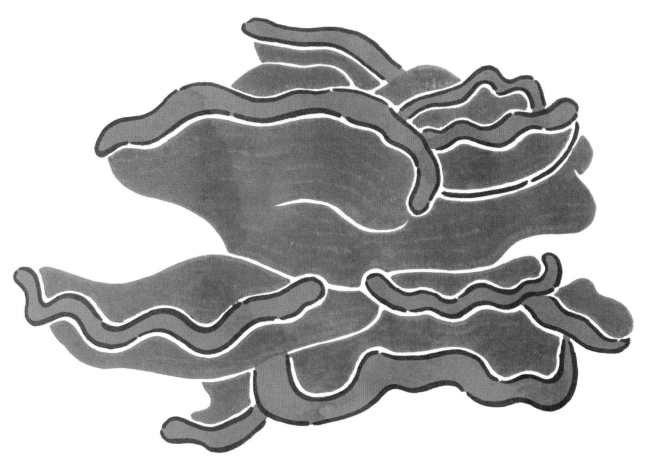

and Chicken Fungus.
(LAETIPOROUS SULPHUREUS)

TRUFFLES

We are ignored,
stepped on, and
often never seen.

We can delight your
taste buds, if you eat us.

And we can displease your
stomach, if you eat us.

We feed on dead things,
and we feed on living things.

We are kind and polite,
and we are friends of the trees.

We are selfish and rude,
and we are enemies of the trees.

MYCORRHIZAL

SYMBIOTIC

SAPROTROPHIC

PARASITIC

We keep growing and
spreading our fingers
to connect the plants
beneath the Earth.

We keep growing

and spreading ourselves

to takeover the
depths of the Earth.

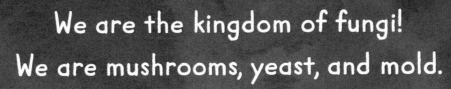

We are the kingdom of fungi!
We are mushrooms, yeast, and mold.

We are fungi!

And now you are one of us.

Glossary

Armillaria solidipes: See Honey Fungus colony in Oregon.

Bioluminescence: Some organisms can glow in the dark, caused by chemical reactions.

Bleeding Tooth: *(Hydnellum peckii)* A fungus that when young, makes a red liquid that oozes out holes in the cap, like blood droplets. They turn brown with age.

Bolete: A general category of fungus known for its cap that sticks out over its stalk, with a spongy surface under its cap instead of gills.

Brain Mushroom: *(Gyromitra esculenta)* A fungus known for its brain-shaped cap.

Cap: The top part of many fungi that often resembles an umbrella top and holds all the spores.

Chicken Fungus: *(Laetiporus sulphureus)* A fungus known for growing as shelves on trees, and for its orange color with lighter edges.

Coprophilous fungi: These fungi often grow on animal poop. They shoot out their spores, which can land on plants nearby. An animal eats the plant (and the spores), poops them both out, and then spores grow mushrooms out of the poop.

Fairy ring: A circle of mushrooms whose cause is not completely understood. They are seen as magical in folklore.

Fruiting body: The part of a fungus that makes spores. If the fruiting body grows above the soil, it is often called a mushroom or mold. The fruiting body is only one part of the life cycle of a fungi, and not the entire organism.

Fungi: Organisms that include yeast, mold, and mushrooms. They are not plants or animals. They eat by decomposing and digesting nutrients in the soil.

Gills: Ribs under the cap of fruiting bodies, used to spread spores, and important in identification.

Gyromitra esculenta: See Brain Mushroom.

Hericium erinaceus: See Lion's Mane Mushroom.

Honey Fungus colony in Oregon: *(Armillaria solidipes)* A member of this species is the largest living organism in the world, spreading over 2.4 square miles in Oregon, and is over 2,400 years old!

Hydnellum peckii: See Bleeding Tooth.

Jelly Fungi: Many types of fungi known for their jelly-like, rubbery fruiting bodies. The fungi shrivel up when dry, but plump back up when they touch water.

Kingdom: Part of the way organisms are classified in biology. Kingdoms are the second highest level, and there are six kingdoms: Animalia, Plantae, Fungi, Protista, Archaea, and Bacteria.

Laetiporus sulphureus: See Chicken Fungus.

Lemon Yellow Lepiota: *(Leucocoprinus birnbaumii)* A small, poisonous fungus known for its yellow color, tall umbrella-like cap, and gills under the cap.

Leucocoprinus birnbaumii: See Lemon Yellow Lepiota.

Lion's Mane Mushroom: *(Hericium erinaceus)* A fungus known for its long quills that grow in clumps.

Mold: A type of multicellular fungus that grows in branches called hyphae, and is known for looking fluffy or fuzzy. It often grows on old, forgotten food.

Mushroom: The fruiting body of a fungus that grows above ground and makes spores. The word mushroom is culturally used to describe the entire organism, but is actually just one part of a larger fungus.

Mushroom hunting dog: Various dog breeds are bred for hunting mushrooms, including truffles and morels, which grow under dead leaves and are difficult for humans to see. The dogs can find them using their sense of smell. Some hunters prefer to use pigs instead of dogs, although they sometimes eat the mushrooms.

Glossary

Mycelia: The part of a fungus with a group of branches called hyphae, which absorb nutrients from the soil. When two mycelium match and connect, they can join and make fruiting bodies, like mushrooms. The mycelia put out enzymes that break down the molecules in the soil around them, and then they absorb the nutrients. This is how the fungus eats.

Mycology: The study of fungi.

Mycorrhizal: A type of relationship between two organisms, like fungi and roots of a plant. The relationship is often beneficial for both organisms (mutualistic), like sharing nutrients.

Parasitic: A negative type of relationship between two organisms, like fungi and roots of a plant. It is usually beneficial for one organism (the parasite), and detrimental for the other (the host).

Phallus indusiatus: See Veiled Lady.

Pink Oyster Mushroom: *(Pleurotus djamor)* A fungus known for its oyster-like shape, with curled edges, and bright pink color.

Pleurotus djamor: See Pink Oyster Mushroom.

Puffball: A category of fungi known for its round shape with no cap or stalk. The spores are made inside the ball, then the ball dries up and splits open, releasing a brown dust cloud full of spores into the air.

Saprotrophic: Getting nutrients by breaking down and digesting dead or decayed matter.

Spore: A cell made by fungi, plants, and protozoa to reproduce. In fungi, the spores are made inside the fruiting body, and are spread by wind or animals. They are similar to a seed, but are only one cell, while a seed is made of many cells.

Stalk: The part of a mushroom that sprouts up from the soil and holds the cap. The stalk holds the cap above the ground so the spores can spread out farther. Not all mushrooms have stalks.

Symbiotic: A long-term, entwined relationship between two organisms, like fungi and roots of a plant. The relationship can be mutualistic or parasitic.

Toe fungus: A fungus that infects toenails or fingernails, causing the nail to thicken and become yellow, white, black, or green. If not treated, the nail can fall off completely.

Truffle: *(Tuber spp.)* A type of mushroom that is known for its rock-like shape and strong flavor. Truffles are hunted by dogs and pigs and sold to chefs and foodies for extremely high prices.

Veiled Lady: *(Phallus indusiatus)* A fungus known for its small cone shaped cap, thick stalk, and lace-like veil hanging from the cap down to the bottom of the stalk.

Yeast: A type of fungi that is a unicellular (single-celled) microorganism. Some yeasts cause fermentation, some cause infections in humans, and some are used to make biofuels.

Bibliography

Marley, Greg. *Chanterelle Dreams, Amanita Nightmares: The Love, Lore, and Mystique of Mushrooms.* White River Junction: Chelsea Green Publishing Company, 2010.

Bone, Eugenia. *Mycophilia: Revelations from the Weird World of Mushrooms.* New York: Rodale Inc., 2011.

Petersen, Jens H. *The Kingdom of Fungi.* Princeton: Princeton University Press, 2013.

Wikipedia Contributors. *Portal: Fungi.* Wikipedia, The Free Encyclopedia. Wikipedia, The Free Encyclopedia. 25 Jan. 2015. Web. 15 Jan. 2016. <https://en.wikipedia.org/wiki/Portal:Fungi>

Ching, Barbara. *NAMA Education Resources.* North American Mycological Association, 15 Jan. 2016. <http://www.namyco.org/education.php>

Willis, Katherine J. *The Importance of Fungi.* Royal Botanic Gardens, Kew, 15 Jan. 2016. <http://www.kew.org/importance-fungi>

Might Could Beta Books

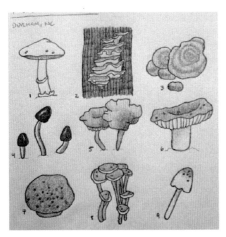  

Thank you members!

This book would not have been possible without the encouragement, feedback, and contributions from the members of Might Could Beta Books. This group of readers, writers, and artists helped me create the book now in your hands, and it's a far better book because of them!

Thank you to all the Might Could Beta Book members for your thoughts, suggestions, and support! Now let's get started on the next book!

Anna McGregor
Camille Medina
Chad Behnke
Chris Silvestre
Emma Bushi
Heidi Eichenberger
Howell Burnell
Ina Wienesen
Jennifer Mandel

Joy Manoleros
Julie Stancato
Kristin Morin
Laura Searle
Lisa Glanz
Lise Demoulin
Natalia Nikulina
Toni Douglas

To learn more about this group, become a member, and be a part of my live book making process, visit the Might Could Beta Books page on my website: www.mightcouldstudios.com

About the Author

Hi! I'm Christine Nishiyama, an illustrator and writer currently living in Atlanta. I create stories, books, and comics that blend fiction and nonfiction. I love researching, writing, and drawing things I don't understand, coming out on the other end of the process with a greater appreciation of just how weird the world is. I also teach art courses to encourage more people to make books and art!

Learn more:
www.mightcouldstudios.com

See more of my process:
@might_could
#MightCouldMushroom

Get a free fungi activity guide:
www.mightcouldstudios.com/wearefungi

Want to give me feedback or just say hello?
Email me at christine@mightcouldstudios.com

Thanks for reading!

Made in the USA
Monee, IL
18 September 2020